On 24 August 79 AD, the volcano Vesuvius, which had remained without noticeable activity for many centuries, exploded with tremendous force. The eruption inundated the vineyards on the mountain slopes with lava, and buried the cities of Pompeii and Stabiae deep in ashes and grit, and the city of Herculaneum beneath a sea of mud. For nearly seventeen centuries all trace of the busy life of these settlements was lost; and it is only in the last century that we have really begun to understand the architecture, the administration and the daily round of these cities of Vesuvius.

POMPEII

Historical Background

The southern face of Vesuvius slopes down to the Sarno valley in a succession of small hills of lava, planted with vineyards; on one of these hills stands the ancient town of Pompeii. The place was particularly favourable for the development of a town engaged in agriculture, trade and industry as they were conceived in classical times. Indeed, it was located in one of the most fertile regions of Italy; open to trade with bigger and richer neighbouring towns in Campania, and at the same time near the sea. We know that Pompeii was considered the natural port of Nola, Nuceria and Acerra, although today it is difficult to recognise both the old coastline, which was then nearer the town, and the position of the port, which must have been formed by the Sarno estuary itself.

From what we know of ancient Campania and considering the means at our disposal to reconstruct it, we can say that Pompeii was founded by the Oscans during the eighth century BC. It was influenced by neighbouring Greek colonies which settled in the sixth century BC, and by Cuma in particular; this is also borne out by a temple of Greek style dating from 550 BC. This is the Doric temple located on the Triangular Forum.

Rare terracotta architecture preserved in the huge cemetery also indicates an Etruscan influence. In fact, Pompeii had close relations with the Etruscan world in its oldest period, competing with the local Greek population for a long time for supremacy in the region. The area inhabited at this time included the district surrounding the Forum square, with square blocks of houses and straight roads, as well as the district of the Triangular Forum. City walls marked the boundary of a wider urban area which was increasingly occupied by buildings until Roman times.

This was the appearance, both complex and ordered, of Pompeii (an appearance worthy of more research and further clarification on the part of scholars) when, towards the middle of the fifth century BC, Samnites from the countryside poured into Campania and settled almost everywhere.

The Samnite Period

Although it is impossible to fix a precise date, it is thought that the Samnite period of the town began around 425 BC. The history of Pompeii, as we know it, is rather poor in literary sources; the town is rarely mentioned in classical texts. We know of only one event of this period which relates to the Samnite wars. In 310, P. Cornelius, charged by the Romans to assure the control of the 'marine coast', set off from Ostia and came to Pompeii, where he recruited a party of allies from the region of Campania; he then marched on Nuceria Alfaterna and sacked it. But, during their return to their ships, his troops were attacked and had to abandon their booty. With hostilities at an end, Pompeii remained a faithful ally of Rome and was loyal even during the troubles years of the Punic wars. It kept, however, its administrative autonomy, its magistrates, its language and economic and commercial independence. Samnite Pompeii enjoyed a period of prosperity and urban expansion and had a high standard of artistic appreciation. The boundary walls were re-sited and, on the perimeter, new districts were created with wide, straight roads and huge blocks of houses.

It is at this time that the main public buildings were erected or re-designed. The Triangular Forum was developed with a monumental entrance with Ionic columns, and a Doric colonnade around the area, while the former Doric temple in the centre was rebuilt. Nearby, a theatre had been built in a natural hollow of the hillside, and next to it stands the Odeon. The latter dates from 80 BC and today still has its old, harmonious appearance with its compact perspectives, and is very evocative of ancient Pompeii because of its good state of preservation and the elegance of its ornamental work. Behind the theatre toward the Forum there is a small gymnasium where a replica of the Doryphore of Polyclete was discovered.

The Forum square was embellished with porticos of Doric columns and perhaps it was enlarged. On the right hand side there is a temple to Jupiter; to the west, the temple of Apollo was restored and a basilica was built. Apart from later additions, this dates from the latter half of the second century BC and is also the oldest building of its type known to us. The interior must have been vast and open, surrounded by a portico with the tribunal behind.

The House of the Faun

There are many examples of the private residence: a vast *domus* with an *atrium*, elegantly and solidly constructed, with refined ornamentation. The House of the Faun is justly famous in this respect. Recent excavations have revealed a previous dwelling on its site, going back to the fifth century BC. But the present appearance of the house, dating from the second century during the Samnite period which was, as we have said, known for its urban expansion and noble architecture, was strongly influenced by Hellenistic art.

The entrance opens on to the Nolan Way and the vestibule, decorated with two shrines to the Lares, leads into the great *atrium*. There, the walls are decorated in the severe first Pompeiian style (as are the other parts of the house) and the *impluvium* is ornamented with a little bronze figure of a faun, of Greek origin of the third to the second centuries BC. Around the *atrium* are the bedrooms; at the back is the *tablinum* with two *triclinia* with mosaic decorations: a marine faun and Dionysos astride a panther. (The mosaics of the house are now in the Naples Museum). To the right of the *atrium* is another set of rooms, perhaps reserved for the owners, with a second *atrium* surrounded by bedrooms. Behind this section of the house, there is a first peristyle with an Ionic portico. On one side are the domestic quarters and, at the back, two *triclinia* (dining rooms) and a sitting room with its floor covered in the famous mosaic of the Battle of Issus. Next, there is a second, much bigger peristyle with a Doric portico. Few, but definite, remains indicate the existence of another floor. It is, therefore, a particularly vast and sumptuous residence, with sophisticated decoration and a rational

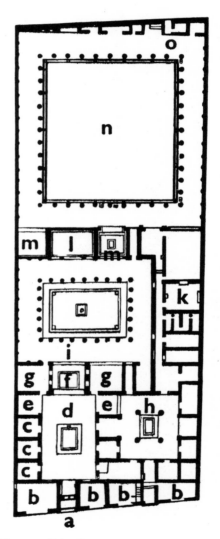

The House of the Faun

a: *Entrance*   **b:** *Shops*   **c:** *Bedrooms*
d: *Atrium*   **e:** *Wings*   **f:** *Tablinum*
g: *Triclinium*   **h:** *Atrium*   **i:** *Peristyle*
j: *Baths*   **k:** *Kitchen*   **l:** *Sitting-room with mosaic of the Battle of Issus*   **m:** *Triclinium*
n: *Great peristyle*   **o:** *Rear entrance*

and complex layout, where the plan of the former Italian house has been embellished with harmonious peristyles of Hellenistic inspiration.

The House of C. Julius Polybius

The house of C. Julius Polybius seems to be of the same period as the House of the Faun and has been the object of systematic excavation. Beyond the austere facade a small but high *atrium* has been discovered. The walls are decorated in the first style; renovation began after the earthquake of 62 and was not completed; there is a false, painted door, a rare and remarkable example of its kind. Beside it, there is a second *atrium* and the other rooms, which are on two storeys, are slowly being unearthed. In conclusion, buildings of the Samnite period, which have survived later renovations, clearly show the influence of Hellenistic art, revealed not only by the architecture, but also by its mural decoration, mosaics and sculptures. Works of art, sometimes imported from Greece, are most commonly of local manufacture, but always refined and of good taste.

The last years of Samnite Pompeii saw the upheavals and battles of civil war. In 89 BC, during the occupation by Lucius Cluentius's troops, the town was besieged and captured by Sulla. Excavations have brought to light interesting evidence of this dramatic event. The so-called "eituns", painted inscriptions in the Samnite language, indicate posts assigned to each group of defenders. Pompeii became a Roman colony in 80 BC and took its name of Colonia Veneria Cornelia Pompeiorum, an obvious allusion to the dictator who had conquered it and to his own divine protector.

The Roman Period

Pompeii, governed by the usual colonial system from this time on, forms a part of the vast history of Rome. Life must have been peaceful with occasional outbursts of local political activity, of which we can form a vivid impression because of the inscriptions which can still be read today on the walls of houses.

From this period, one incident has been recorded; in the year 59 AD, a scuffle broke out between Pompeiians and Nucerians in the amphitheatre and led to the suspension of all spectacles for ten years by order of the Senate. But

contact with Rome and internal activity led, inevitably, to the evolution of social structure in the town. The old Pompeiian families, and those settled after the romanisation of the region, acquired their wealth primarily from agriculture and land. During the course of the first century AD, there was a tendency towards industrial development as this was understood in ancient Rome. Because of this development, town planning underwent changes. Shops and workshops forming a part of some houses occupy an ever increasing place. Many of these businesses were run, not by free craftsmen, but by slaves and freedmen.

However it would seem that there was no radical social change, but merely a change of activity on the part of families who already had political and social power. It cannot be said whether it was the result of an 'industrial revolution', or if this change took a long time to evolve. It is only known that the development accelerated in the final years of Pompeii, between the earthquake of the year 62 and the fatal eruption.

The *pax romana* and close contact with Rome entailed a substantial renewal in the field of public and private construction; new additions were made, sometimes even replacing those previously of Hellenistic influence. The town was embellished by the restoration of the Forum, the temple of Jupiter, theatres and other public buildings. A temple in honour of Augustus was built, another for Vespasian; the impressive building of Eumachia and the Great Gymnasium were built in this period. Houses also benefitted from the artistic movement: new trends can be seen in wall paintings and various ornamental styles which followed. At the same time, beside the old type of *domus* of Italian origin, houses of less architectural interest, but which were more functional, appeared and these were better suited to new social and economic needs. Wealth sometimes got the better of good taste, allowing the figurative arts to flourish in quantity (but also often in quality), sometimes giving birth to a local style, sometimes following the eclectic style and attitudes of the capital.

The Warning Signs

In the year 62, as we have said, Pompeii was shaken by an earthquake, causing serious damage. Tacitus and Seneca mention it in their writings, and the traces are still visible on all or almost all the buildings in the town. The amount of reconstruction necessary proved to be enormous and could not be done well in a short period of time. The smallest houses, shops and businesses were promptly restored but in the large elegant residences restoration was slow. The urban administration multiplied its efforts to repair the Forum, temples, theatres and all other public buildings, but work was still in progress when the eruption occurred.

The Tragedy

The Romans had only a vague idea of the volcanic nature of Vesuvius; they were used to considering it as a verdant mountain, where thick woods alternated with fertile vineyards. On August 24 in the year 79 (the date given by Pliny), the mountain awoke; in two days it engulfed a huge area of the countriside in a downpour of ash and grit, destroying villages and towns in its wake. The catastrophe was dreadful. Those who could not find shelter in time fell victim to volcanic matter, especially to the deadly fumes which spread everywhere.

A vivid and moving description is given in two letters from Pliny to Tacitus, informing the Roman historian of the death of his uncle, Pliny the Elder. The latter at that time commanded the fleet at Messina; having seen the eruption from the distance, he went towards it, either out

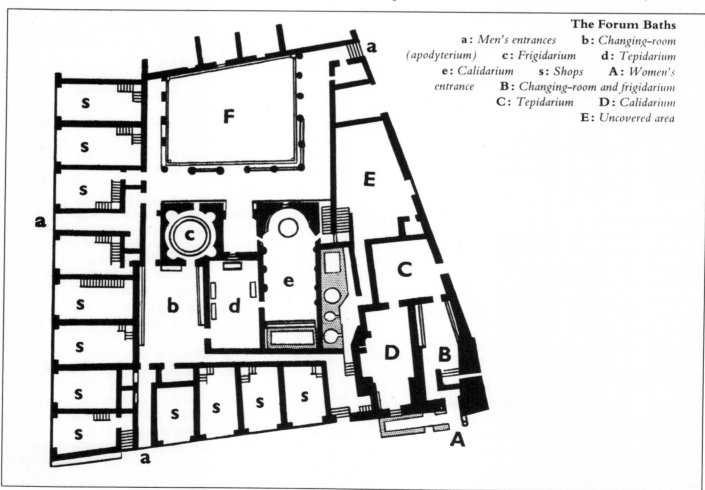

The Forum Baths
a: *Men's entrances*   **b:** *Changing-room (apodyterium)*   **c:** *Frigidarium*   **d:** *Tepidarium*   **e:** *Calidarium*   **s:** *Shops*   **A:** *Women's entrance*   **B:** *Changing-room and frigidarium*   **C:** *Tepidarium*   **D:** *Calidarium*   **E:** *Uncovered area*

of curiosity as a man of science, or to try and help in some way, but he, too, fell a victim.

The letters of Pliny are dramatically confirmed by the bodies of the unfortunate inhabitants, in the most moving postures, seized by death at the moment of trying desperately to flee, attempting to protect themselves from the noxious fumes with a piece of their clothing, or carrying away with them a precious object or a sum of money. Pompeii was covered to a depth of more than 6 metres (20 feet) and only the upper part of buildings remained visible above the blanket of volcanic matter. Everywhere was deserted: only occasionally a few survivors came back to pillage or recover goods.

Contemporaries were deeply affected by the tragedy: Martial and Stacius recall it in lines full of emotion; the emperor Titus commended the assistance that had been given. The event continued to be evoked much later, not only by Latin writers such as Boccaccio, but even more by the Italian humanists, from Petrarch to Pontano and Sannazzaro.

The site itself, at least from the Middle Ages on, was called Civita, a common name in southern Italy for places inhabited in ancient times and later abandoned. Nobody thought of identifying ancient Pompeii and even less of looking under the ground.

The Renaissance
The first remains of the buried town were brought to light between 1594 and 1600, when the architect Domenico Fontana made a canal through the region to drain off the water of the Sarno, but did not explore any further. It was only in 1748, ten years after the beginning of excavation in Herculaneum, that research began in Pompeii. It has continued almost without interruption.

Today, therefore, we can see this old town, its scars caused by the earthquake not yet been completely healed, added to which are the ravages of the eruption; nevertheless it appears miraculously intact, better preserved than almost any other archaeological site, precisely because the eruption buried it instantly. Its charm and special interest are also due to the fact that Pompeii is a town where every day excavation brings new information to light: houses still recognizable in their unity, their decoration, their furniture and, between them, the paved streets bearing the traces of chariots, the sidewalks, the public fountains lining roads and squares. To these are added the reproduction, by means of plaster or cement moulds, of the organic elements which were destroyed – corpses of the eruption's victims, wooden objects, doors, chariot wheels and tree trunks. We find also, on the plaster of the houses, electoral slogans painted in bright colours, short poems, caricatures and obscene comments. The shops still have their painted signs and various utensils arranged on the counters; workshops are recognisable by their tools. Houses have kept their mural decoration and objects of everyday use which allow us to experience the intimacy of family life two thousand years ago.

From the numerous portraits recovered, we are familiar with the physiognomy of Pompeiian men and women; their actions, customs and ambitions have been revealed to us by all manner of documents.

Pompeii in the First Century of the Empire
Let us try to gain a general view of Pompeii in the first century of the Empire, so different from the Samnite town of which we have already spoken.

The district of the Triangular Forum, with its nearby theatres, has not changed; only the former Doric temple is reduced to a simple chapel. The Forum, renovated with its surrounding porticos of travertine and marble, has the Capitol as its background, dedicated to Jupiter, Juno and Minerva, and flanked by triumphal arches. On the west side, starting from the ancient basilica, there are municipal administrative buildings, the office of the *aediles* (building superintendents), the *curia*, the office of the *duumvirs* and the *comitium* where elections were arranged. On the east, there is a huge building which the priestess Eumachia had constructed at her own expense to serve as a seat for one of the most flourishing trades of Pompeii, that of *fullones* (fullers), the makers and dyers of wool cloth. Then comes a small temple, dedicated, it would appear, to the emperor Vespasian; next the sanctuary of the Lares with a great apse at the back; finally, the *macellum*, a large market with shops and a chapel dedicated to the imperial cult.

Beyond the square, and almost behind the temple of Jupiter, stands a temple dedicated to Fortuna Augusta, frequently worshipped in Roman imperial times, and the Forum bath-houses.

On the south-east edge of the town we find the amphitheatre and Great Gymnasium. The amphitheatre of
Pompeii, the oldest one known, was built around 80 BC
during the renovation and development of the town after
its conquest by Sulla and its transformation into a Roman
colony. The elements of later amphitheatres of the imperial
era are absent; there is no underground stage area and the
access staircases to the terraces are placed outside. The
simplicity of its structure makes it, so to speak, severe and
solemn; its monumental character finds a natural comple-
ment in the Great Gymnasium, a huge uncovered area
with a swimming pool in the centre and a portico on three
sides; it was formerly planted with great plane trees.

The Houses

The private buildings are equally important evidence, and
we can cite a few of the most typical examples. The House
of Menander, built on the site of an older house, has a
majestic *atrium* and a beautiful peristyle, around which are
placed the other rooms, a small bath-house and slaves'
quarters. Mural decorations, of the fourth Pompeiian
style, as well as the mosaic floors, are important. They
reveal wealth and good taste in the houses called the
House of Golden Cupids, the House of the Silver Wedding,
the House of the Cryptoporticus, and the House of the
Labyrinth, of which recent restoration and preservation
work has increased the interest. Better known still, and
justly so, is the House of the Vettii, with its beautiful
garden decorated with small statues, ponds, fountains and
a large dining room with rich and fantastic ornamental
cupids, maenads and satyrs. At the far end of the house, in
the *Via dell' Abbondanza*, certain houses seem to lose their
residential character in their design and by the predomin-
ance of open air spaces. The elegant House of the Marine
Venus has a peristyle showing the goddess surrounded by
garden scenes. In the house of Loreius Tiburtinus, the
garden is more important than the living quarters. Rooms
are spread around the *atrium*, with a mural decoration of
great beauty but, at the back, where the peristyle has been
abandoned, there is a long uncovered pergola overlooking
the *triclinium* and a huge *hortus*, both decorated with
paintings, chapels and small statues scattered in the
greenery. The nearby villa of Julia Felix is still *intra muros*,
but could be said to lead towards the countryside beyond.

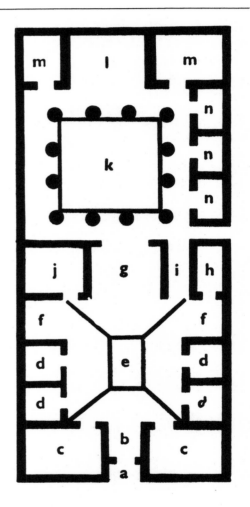

Typical plan of a Pompeiian house
a: *Vestibule*   **,b:** *Inner vestibule (fauces)*
c: *Side rooms (cellae)*   **d:** *Bedrooms (cubicula)*
e: *Atrium*   **f:** *Wings (alae)*   **g:** *Tablinum*
h: *Store-room (apotheca)*   **i:** *Corridor (andron)*
j: *Triclinium*   **k:** *Peristyle*   **l:** *Sitting-room
(exedra)*   **m:** *Inner rooms (oeci)*
n: *Bedrooms (cubicula)*

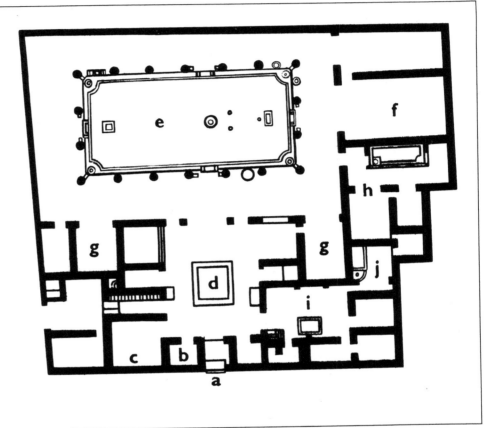

The House of the Vettii
a: *Entrance*   **b:** *Side room (cella)*
c: *Inner room (oecus) of the atrium*
d: *Atrium*   **e:** *Peristyle*
f: *Large dining-room (triclinium)*
g: *Inner rooms (oeci) of the peristyle*
h: *Women's appartments*
i: *Little atrium with altar to the Lares*
j: *Kitchen*

Large villas are in general scattered about the countryside, according to the position of the farms and residences of which, in some way, they constitute the nervecentre. But others have been found on the edge of Pompeii itself. The villa of Fabius Rufus is only partially unearthed; those of Diomedes, and of Cicero, and the Villa of Mosaic Columns, situated outside the Herculanean Gate, are better known. But the most interesting is the Villa of Mysteries, renowned for the pictorial cycle which has given it its name.

The Villa of Mysteries

The part situated near the entrance (still not fully unearthed), is occupied by farm quarters, with kitchen, bakery and oven, wine-cellar and a place for a wine-press. The accommodation of the occupiers is set around the *atrium* and the *tablinum*. Near the latter, there is the *triclinium* with its great fresco. This is the work of an artist from Campania of the middle of the first century and the fresco is strongly influenced by the figurative themes of the Hellenistic period. The interpretation given today to this type of pictorial cycle, which entirely covers the walls of the room, is neither convincing nor accurate. It is certain, however, that this painting bears some relation to a mysterious cult; it has been said that it represents different phases in the initiation of a wife into the mysteries of Dionysos. Beginning with a child reading the ritual, there follow scenes of sacrifice and symbolic flagellation, and a young woman washing herself. She gets dressed, solemnly puts on a coat and sits down. She is then initiated into the mysteries of the god.

In the new found peace of the Empire, the boundary walls no longer have a defensive purpose; they are merely the witnesses of the past. But, if the town does not yet extend beyond their perimeter, new houses are rising and using the same foundations, as can be seen near the Marine Gate (it is the same in Herculaneum). Outside the walls, following the custom of the time, extends the cemetery. The Street of Tombs, beyond the Herculanean Gate, has been known for a long time, as well as the tombs of the Gates of Vesuvius and Nola. Monuments of various architectural shapes stand in rows along the roads: columbaria, chapels, little mausolea, whose variety is a valuable contribution to the history of art. The walls are decorated with stucco and paintings, generally relating to the life of the deceased; inscriptions and sculptures tell us his name, his public office and his appearance. There are as many details here about the Pompeiians as in the ruins of their buried town. We can trace their lives, from childhood (since the walls are covered with scholastic exercises or caricatures), passing through youth (inspiring declarations of love or obscenities), and reaching maturity. They then become municipal magistrates, attracting public honours for their administration, or else merchants or bankers creating new fortunes and preserving family prosperity. The funeral building ends their adventure on earth and we can read there the sad homage of their relatives and friends. In Pompeii this dialogue between life and death still seems present, and is perhaps the reason for the subtle charm which it exerts on the visitor.

HERCULANEUM

Historical Background

Ancient Herculaneum lies slightly above sea level, in the curve of the Bay of Naples, on the slopes of Vesuvius and not far from the cities of Campania. Its location has been identified not only by archaeological excavation, which has been bringing information to light for more than two hundred years, but also by references to it in ancient times by poets, writers and geographers. Of particular importance is the *Tabula Peutingeriana*, a large map of the Roman Empire which, although drawn up a few centuries later, shows the position of Herculaneum, as it does other towns

buried by the eruption of Vesuvius in 79 AD. The town was flanked on either side by two rivers flowing down Vesuvius, and it boasted a safe port.

According to legend, Herculaneum was founded by Hercules – hence its name – at the time of the hero's return from his journey to Iberia. In fact, the results of excavation offer fewer clues about the early history of Herculaneum than at nearby Pompeii. However an Oscan settlement must have been established here, and there was immigration from neighbouring Greek colonies, especially Cuma and Neapolis and, to a certain extent, from the Etruscan district of Capua. With the occupation of Campania by the Samnites in the latter half of the fifth century BC, Herculaneum too became a Samnite town and thus it remained until the end of the war between Rome and the Samnites.

We know that Herculaneum took part in the rebellion of the Italian populace against Rome, which was finally put down in 89 BC by Titus Didus, one of Sulla's lieutenants and, after losing all political autonomy, Herculaneum became a Roman *municipium*.

Throughout the rest of its existence, the town had no events of historical importance and remained one of the many small centres of the Empire, but it was a popular resort among noble and wealthy Romans, and later among members of the imperial household, for its climate and scenic beauty, equalling other resorts in the Bay of Naples. Then, in the year 62, it was one of the towns damaged by the earthquake and, later, in the year 79, was buried by the eruption of Vesuvius.

Heavy rains accompanying the eruption caused a flow of muddy lava which completely submerged the town. In time, the semi-liquid matter solidified and formed a thick bank, resembling tufa; the earth level rose by an average of 15 metres (50 feet). Although, on the one hand, the mural foundations were damaged by the burial and a great number of things were washed away and lost in the violence of the torrent; on the other hand, things remained compact and sealed, as it were, in the solid mass, and were thus better preserved. This is why we find that in Herculaneum, more than the other neighbouring towns, organic matter, especially wood, is still in good condition, and why it has been possible to recover the famous papyrus rolls.

General view of the excavations at Herculaneum

The memory of Herculaneum and its dramatic end lasted for a considerable time, particularly in literary and scholastic circles, and a new centre of habitation was established on the site of the buried town in the Middle Ages; it was called Resina, a name of uncertain origin and meaning, until in 1969 it was renamed Herculaneum.

Archaeological Discoveries

The first archaeological discoveries were made at the beginning of the eighteenth century: in 1709, when a well in the wood of Frati Alcantarini was being excavated, the shell of a theatre was found by chance underground.

For several years the Prince of Elbeuf took advantage of the discovery to unearth sculptures and ornate marbles, which were scattered here and there, and it was at that time that the two famous statues called the 'great' and the 'little' Herculanean girl ended up in the Dresden museum. In 1738 regular excavation work was begun, sponsored by king Charles of Bourbon, and this was the first time that systematic exploration of an ancient site occurred. Standards at that time were not the same as today: deep shafts were dug to gain access to the ancient level and it was, therefore, by means of underground tunnels that the substratum was explored, bringing to light whatever was found to arouse scholastic interest, such as inscriptions, statues, pieces of frescoes and a variety of objects. At the

F. A. Mella

A contemporary print of the Bourbon excavations

same time, with remarkable skill and precision and in conditions of great discomfort, the layout of buildings and streets was reconstructed. Work was carried out in this way until 1761, and the findings were of such value that the interest of cultured men in Europe was aroused, beginning with Winckelmann, who stayed there for some time and wrote learned and enthusiastic articles on the subject.

Consider, for instance, the discovery of some of the public buildings and the imposing Pisoni villa, revealing a series of bronze and marble statues and an abundance of Greek papyri containing philosophical tracts. The excavations were led by Alcubierre, Weber and La Vega, and it is to these last two men in particular that we owe the detailed map of the excavation. After a long interruption,

excavation work was resumed in 1828, this time not by underground tunnels, but above ground, and continued, with several stoppages, until 1875. The work was carried out slowly and with many obstacles, not least of which was the presence of Resina standing on the ancient town.

The present phase in the history of Herculaneum's excavation began in 1927 and is still continuing. With technology constantly being adapted to the needs of science, thus broadening the field of interest and research into classical studies, large sections of ancient Herculaneum have come to light. The most interesting results of this period lie, perhaps, in the information on town planning and house design in Herculaneum. Closely linked to archaeological excavation is the delicate and demanding work of restoration, which is essential to prevent further damage to the discoveries and the consequent risk of total destruction.

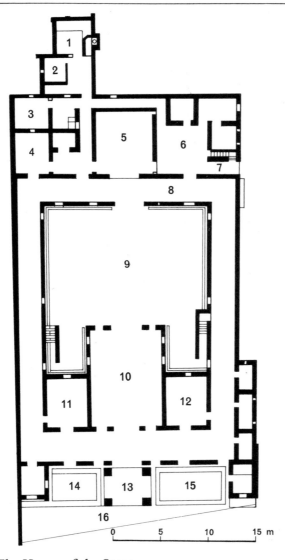

The House of the Stags

1: *Kitchen*   **2**: *Store-room*   **3–4**: *Inner rooms (oeci)*   **5**: *Triclinium*   **6**: *Atrium*

7: *Vestibule*   **8**: *Arcade*   **9**: *Garden*

10: *Large triclinium*   **11–12**: *Living rooms (oeci)*

13: *Pergula*   **14–15**: *Cubicula diurna*

16: *Terrace*

From 1750 onwards, works of art which were recovered in the excavations were collected in the Herculaneum museum, specially created in the royal palace of nearby Portrei, and it was here that the findings of Pompeii and Stabiae were also brought. The Herculaneum and other collections are now in the great Bourbon museum in Naples, where they have been since it was opened at the beginning of the nineteenth century.

Town Planning

Ancient Herculaneum has still not been fully explored. We do know, however, what its town planning system was in the year 79 AD, although we know little or nothing of its development prior to the first century of the Empire. It is thought that the inhabited area measured approximately 37c × 320 metres (400 × 350 yards). It was encircled by a wall with gates and look-out towers; we know only of one stretch on the south side, but there are also inscriptions and literary references to this wall.

The town plan is shown as having streets with intersections at right angles – *decumani* running east to west and *cardines* running north to south – and which run between rectangular buildings, each one differing in extent. The terrain is on a definite, although not very steep, slope. During the last period of its existence, the town expanded to the south; on the southern walls luxurious, beautifully appointed houses were built and, outside the walls, public buildings were constructed, including a place of worship and a large bath-house. Furthermore, the surrounding countryside must have been dotted with country and suburban villas, one of which is the vamous Villa of Papyri (the Pisoni Villa which has already been mentioned). Finally, Herculaneum had a port which has not yet been identified but is known to us from a reference by the historian Dionysius of Halicarnassus.

It seems clear that, contrary to the usual pattern of Italian and Roman cities, the town centre did not have a main square, a Forum, but had instead the *Decumanus Maximus*, running from east to west in the centre of the urban network. This street, wider than any of the others, would have served the same purpose as the Forum and, on certain occasions, would have been closed to traffic. It is certain that some of the main public buildings were here. To the east is the great gymnasium with a monumental

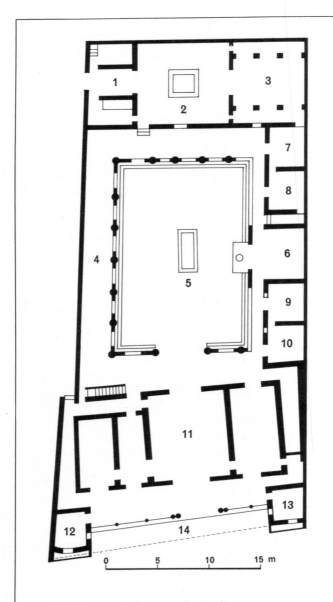

The House of the Mosaic Atrium

1: *Vestibule*   2: *Atrium*   3: *Tablinum*
4: *Arcade*   5: *Garden*   6: *Sitting-room*
7–10: *Bedrooms*   11: *Triclinium*
12–13: *Cubicula diurna*   14: *Colonnade*

entrance on the *decumanus*; to the south there is a building which appears to have been the seat of local magistrates, but also a centre for cultural events, and a large building, only partly excavated, which was probably associated with religion; to the north there is the Basilica which was unearthed in the Bourbon period, known to us by notes and drawings of that time. Other public buildings are situated in various places: the theatre in the north-west; along the *Decumanus Inferior* is the bath-house and outside the walls, to the south, is a place of worship and more bath-houses.

Principal Houses and Shops in Herculaneum
Private houses in Herculaneum are of particular interest in that they reveal a great variety of designs. We find a rare example of a lodging house (the Trellis House) with a small, central courtyard and small, independent apartments on the ground and upper floors. Also typical is the House of the Beautiful Courtyard with an external staircase leading to a second floor.

One of the oldest examples of a house with an *atrium* is the Samnite house, designed in the austere first style. Later designs, dating from the first century of the Empire, are the House of the Bicentenary and the House of the Wooden Partition, both of which are developments of the original type of Herculanean house. In other houses, for instance the House of the Gem, and the House of the Relief of Telephus, prominence has been given to the *atrium*, which is wide and spacious in proportion to the rest of the house; this type probably emulates private houses in Hellenistic Greece. The large, sumptuous villas, panoramically situated on the town's southern perimeter, have an individual character. In the last period of the town's existence, these villas exploited the position of the boundary walls, whose original purpose had by then become superfluous with the peace and security of imperial politics. The houses in question are those of Aristides and the adjacent house of Argus, the House of the Hotel, covering a vast area, the House of the Mosaic Atrium and the House of the Stags. Each one differs in area and design, reflecting the owners' individual requirements and architectural inventiveness, but the houses have one thing in common – a major development in peristyle. In contrast, on the east-west axis of the town, the *atrium* is frequently reduced to minimal proportions. This type of house, although situated inside the town, is closer to the suburban villa in style than to the town house proper.

Shops in Herculaneum are varied and numerous and reflect the many aspects of everyday life. There is one shop in particular from which wooden shelves, amphorae and other utensils, some still containing charred foodstuffs, have been recovered. Along the *Decumanus Maximus* there is a metal workshop with crucibles and melted residues; there is another shop in which a number of glass articles were found, still wrapped in straw. These shops have painted signs on the outside.

The presence of an upper storey, and sometimes even two, is widely evidenced here, and is perhaps due to the deep level of matter which buried the town, rather than to any particular local building style.

Herculaneum had a population of approximately 5,000, according to the most reliable calculations. The town appears to have been a small centre, enjoying a certain affluence, primarily based on agriculture; as the surrounding area of Vesuvius was very fertile, agriculture flourished in the region. We know, too, from what has been discovered that the inhabitants had a high and often sophisticated standard of living and a developed artistic appreciation.

Closely linked to the architecture of private and public buildings in Herculaneum are wall paintings. These essentially belong to the town's last period and correspond to the third and fourth Pompeiian styles; impressive compositions, of marked Hellenistic influence, adorn the Basilica. In private houses, too, there is a high standard of mural painting, both in the decorative work on single walls and in pictures with mythological themes; some of these echo famous works by Greek artists. In this connection, it is worth remembering the rare, if not unique, example of a picture set in a wooden frame, and a series of small pictures painted on marble. In addition, there are four small pictures in the second style, that is, of the earlier Republican period, which aroused the enthusiasm of Winckelmann when they were first discovered.

The sculpture is extremely rich. Firstly, there are sculptures found in the Pisoni Villa, the only surviving example of the private art collections which wealthy Romans loved to have. Bronze and marble sculptures adorn the theatre, the Basilica and many houses. Stucco and mosaics are common and of a high standard. We also have a rare and interesting example of a mural mosaic in the House of Neptune, which gets its name from the subject of the mosaic.

STABIAE

Historical Background
The populated centre known as Stabiae in Roman times is located above an extreme spur of the Lattari mountains where they slope down to the sea. Stabiae is enclosed by the Sarno river valley to the south and east, making it an advantageous site for human occupation and offering a natural defence; the town enjoys an excellent climate and has natural springs from the mountain. The location is also adjacent to an inlet in the Bay of Naples which is suitable for anchorage. A good road network enables communication with the Sorrento peninsula, the interior of the Sarno valley and important towns, such as Nuceria. In this way, Stabiae developed as an outlet to the sea and as a port for Nuceria and the federation of Italian towns around Nuceria (the Nucerian federation).

Stabiae must have been a very ancient town which, in the absence of written sources, we conclude from its burial sites to date as far back as the eighth century BC. From funeral articles with ceramic earthenware of Corinthian style, we can imagine how Stabiae became part of Italy's economic and historical structure, maintaining relations and trade with other Italian, Etruscan and Hellenic towns. Contact with the Greek world must have continued for a long time, because Greek ceramics are found in the burial sites.

Towards the end of the fifth century BC, Stabiae, like the rest of Campania, saw the arrival of the Samnites, and it was at this time that an alliance with Nuceria was made. Later, Stabiae must have been involved in the Samnite wars and suffered the same fate as Nuceria, both in its military operations against Rome and in its capitulation. At the outbreak of the war between the Italian allies and Rome at the beginning of the first century BC, the Nucerian federation remained loyal to Rome, but later went over to the insurgents. We know that in the year 90 BC the Samnite general, Papius Mutilus, conquered Nula and Stabiae, as well as other towns. However, under Sulla's command, the Roman army overcame the enemy in the following year. Having thus ceased to be an urban centre, Stabiae became, in the latter half of the Republic and the first period of the Empire, a holiday resort with vast, luxurious villas where wealthy and influential Romans would come to spend a part of their life.

This was Stabiae when, in 62 AD, the earthquake occurred; and later, in the year 79, the eruption of Vesuvius buried it under the blanket of ash and grit that blotted out Pompeii, Herculaneum and Oplontis. The present town of Castellammare di Stabia was originally founded at the beginning of the Dark Ages near the site of Stabiae's ancient villas. The memory of buried Stabiae was never forgotten and the name soon came to mean the new urban centre.

Archaeological Excavations

Archaeological excavations were begun in Stabiae at the same time as in Herculaneum and Pompeii and were also carried out by means of subterranean passages. Pieces of painted walls of excellent quality were recovered and, as at Herculaneum, a plan of the villas was drawn up. These excavations of the Bourbon period continued until 1782. Archaeological work was resumed in 1951 and has continued uninterruptedly since then, using modern methods and consequently giving valuable results. In recent years, exploration of burial sites in Santa Maria delle Grazie has been added to the other excavations. The burial sites cover a long period of time, from the eighth to the second century BC. Part of the neighbouring area, such as Carmiano, has also been explored and the findings of these excavations are in the local Antiquarium.

The urban plan of Stabiae still presents some unsolved problems and we are as yet unable to locate the exact pre-Roman town centre, much less a town plan. The position of the burial sites indicates that the town was not too far from them, and it must also have been near the harbour. We do, however, have more information about the villas which replaced the urban centre destroyed by Sulla. These villas are on top of a promontory, all next to each other and all enjoying a pleasant outlook and climate. From what we have learnt from recent excavations and those of the Bourbon period, the villas are particularly interesting; the architecture used both nature and the terrain to full advantage. Much of the design is given over to open spaces, peristyles, gardens and terraces. The rooms for everyday life are usually large and comfortable and there are ample bath-houses. Everywhere, the economic well-being of the owners is to be seen. So, too, is artistic taste as reflected in both painted and stucco murals, in the few sculptures that have been recovered and in domestic and luxury furnishings, such as multi-goblets with Egyptian themes.

1

(Previous page)

1: Pompeii: The Nucerian Gate. Only excavated during the last few years, this gateway opens on to the road which leads from Pompeii to Nuceria Alfaterna. Roman stonework has been built on the original foundations. Just outside the gate is a crossroads, the southwestern branch of which is lined with funereal monuments and has only been partially explored.

2: The Nolan Gate. Built from tufa-rock, it is decorated at the crown by a statue of Minerva. From this point began the road leading to Nola; this was also lined with tombs, as can be seen from the small part which has so far been uncovered.

3: The Herculanean Gate. Its old name was *Porta Salinensis*. This gate was so called because it led not only on to the road to Herculaneum, but also to the coast-road where the salt-works were. Today it stands as it was after modification by the Romans, with three arches to separate traffic from pedestrians. The 'Street of Tombs' which lies beyond this gate is one of the places most typical of ancient Pompeii.

4: **Tower of the Street of Mercury.** The walls of Pompeii were flanked by square towers, the best example of which is tower XI, standing at the end of the *Via di Mercurio*. Built a little before the reign of Sulla in 89 BC, this is one of the town's oldest gates.

5: **The City Walls.** The walls of Pompeii show different methods of construction which date from Samnite and pre-Samnite times, at the beginning of the fifth century BC, up to the last years of its independence before its conquest by L. Cornelius Sulla (89 BC). The earlier constructions using blocks show signs, in several places, of restoration by dry-stone work. Here and there are traces of damage evidently caused by stone missiles launched during the siege by Sulla.

4

5

6

6: Pompeii has kept intact its urban network of streets, as it stood at the time of the eruption. Our photograph shows the roadway paved with huge irregular blocks of stone, and the sidewalks with their stone kerbs. Stones were placed at intervals along the road to allow pedestrians to cross without getting wet on rainy days, since Pompeii had few gutters and the water ran freely along the roads. Also worth noting is a protective block at the corner of the crossroads and, at the entrance to the side-street, a stone placed in the centre to prevent wagons from entering. Fountains were placed along the roads and the entrances to shops and houses opened on to the streets.

7: **The City Bakeries.** Many bakeries have been found in Pompeii. The one situated in the *Vicolo storto* (the crooked lane) is typical. The lava millstones, the oven and the remains of the counter where the bread was laid out can still be seen, exemplifying the different stages of bread making in Pompeii.

7

8

9

8: Electoral Propaganda. The outer walls of houses in Pompeii are covered with electoral slogans – inscriptions painted in red. One can read the names of the candidates who were standing for different municipal posts, or of the communities presenting them to the voters. These are sometimes accompanied by short passages exhorting people to vote.

9: The public fountains in Pompeii are all of the same kind: a square bowl and a water spout usually decorated with a simple motif. The wear and tear on the edges of the bowls shows how much they were used by the citizens.

10–11: Streets. Characteristic and well preserved streets of Pompeii as seen from different angles. Note the tracks worn in the paving by the continuous passing of vehicles.

10   11

12 13

14

15

12: A fountain spout decorated with a symbol of Plenty.

13: Another fountain spout, decorated this time by a cock with outspread wings.

14: **Castellum aquae** (the water tower). Near the Vesuvian Gate is the best example of the reservoirs and conduits regulating the town's water supply, which was brought by the Serino aquaduct (Augustan era).

15: **The Forum.** The Forum was the centre of city life. Shows, games and the most important ceremonies took place there. It is a rectangular square paved with travertine and lined on three sides by a portico. Access for vehicles is prevented by barriers and here one finds the *suggestum* or speakers' platform and the plinths which supported the statues of members of the royal family and well-known citizens. All around stand the main public, civil and religious monuments. At the back on the north side are two triumphal arches, one on each side of the Temple of Jupiter.

16–17: The colonnade surrounding the Forum is not a single construction. On the south side are remains of an older colonnade of the Samnite era and on the west side a travertine portico on two levels, a restoration from the period of Roman imperialism. Numerous other buildings are also faced with a portico. The one before the *macellum* (provision market) is very elegant and has columns with Corinthian capitals.

18: The Temple of Jupiter. The most important temple in the town from the time of its first construction during the Samnite era. During Roman times it became the Capitol. It stands on a high podium with an Etrusco-Italian flight of steps in front. Underneath the podium lie the rooms used for guarding the city treasure and receiving the thank-offerings.

19: Via del Foro. A large road leading from the Forum to the Nolan Way. It is here that the temple of Fortuna Augusta stands.

20: The Temple of Apollo. A religious monument dating as far back as the sixth century BC, although it was last restored during Roman times. This sacred place is surrounded by a wall with a colonnade on three sides. The temple is built in the Etrusco-Italian style. In front is the altar with its dedicatory inscription.

21: The Basilica. Situated next to the Forum Square, it was the centre of both commercial and judiciary life. It dates back to the eleventh century BC and comprises a central open-air site surrounded by a portico with, at the back, the Tribunal.

22: The Temple of Vespasian. This small monument is situated in a sacred precinct and is notable for its marble altar which depicts scenes of sacrifice.

23: Macellum. A large market which was built during the first century of the Empire; the entrance from the Forum opens into an open-air area which is surrounded by arcades, shops and a chapel dedicated to the imperial cult.

24: The Building of Eumachia. This was the centre of the fuller's guild. Built by the priestess Eumachia, it has a very beautiful marble door decorated by motifs depicting plants and vegetables, dating from the first decades of the Empire.

25–26: Triangular Forum. So-called because of its shape, this is a very old building. Its stately entrance and the portico which surrounds it date from the Samnite era; it is the entrance to the Samnite gymnasium and to the Grand Theatre. A marble basin inscribed with a dedication, a round shrine and a semi-circular bench are among the remains.

27: The Doric Temple. This lies at the centre of the Triangular Forum, dates from the middle of the sixth century BC and was probably dedicated to Hercules. It was built according to the rules used for Greek temples and although it was restored during the Samnite era it was partially destroyed during Roman times. Only a simple chapel dedicated to Hercules and Minerva remains.

28: The Temple of Isis. Dedicated to a foreign cult, this was entirely rebuilt after the earthquake of 62. It is well preserved and worthy of note because of its architecture, its stucco and painted decorations and the sacred objects which were found there.

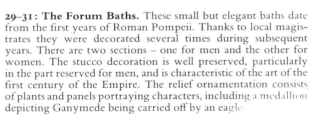

30

29–31: The Forum Baths. These small but elegant baths date from the first years of Roman Pompeii. Thanks to local magistrates they were decorated several times during subsequent years. There are two sections – one for men and the other for women. The stucco decoration is well preserved, particularly in the part reserved for men, and is characteristic of the art of the first century of the Empire. The relief ornamentation consists of plants and panels portraying characters, including a medallion depicting Ganymede being carried off by an eagle.

32–34: The Stabian Baths. The oldest baths in Pompeii which are situated at the cross-roads of the Stabian Way and the *Via dell' Abbondanza.* At least five successive phases of its construction since the second century BC are clearly visible. Rebuilt and enlarged during Roman times, these baths are one of the best examples of this kind of public building, which was widespread in the Roman world. The oldest part consists of small, low rooms and is reached by crossing a large palestra surrounded by arches. On the other side are more recent buildings for men and women, each with a hall, *frigidarium, tepidarium* and *calidarium.* Several of these rooms have stucco decorations which consist of fantastic motifs and different characters taken from the last years of the life of Pompeii. They are among the most beautiful decorations of this kind that have been found.

32

34

35: The Gladiators' Barracks. A large, square court surrounded by a portico behind which are two storeys of small cells. Originally it was a place of rest for spectators from neighbouring theatres; later it was used as a barracks for gladiators, as the many arms which can be found there bear witness.

36: The Theatre. The early works probably date from the fifth century BC, with the *cavea* using the natural slope of the land. Later alterations were made and the tiers, the stage and dais were built. It stands today as it has been since the first century of our era and has all the characteristics of the Roman theatre. It was open-air but under certain circumstances could be covered with a *velarium*. It held about five thousand spectators.

37

38

37: The Odeon. Built about 80 years BC, this was used for concerts, plays and mimes. It was covered by a wooden roof and did not hold more than a thousand spectators. Its structure and decoration are very elegant.

38: The entrance to the Odeon from the Stabian Way.

39: Theatrical Mask. One of the numerous relief representations of theatrical history and life that can be found in Pompeii.

46: The House of Pansa. This dates from the Samnite era and has a huge garden spreading out from the peristyle. It was originally much larger, but its owner changed a part into small apartments for renting.

47: House of L. Caius Secundus. The front is still decorated in the first Pompeiian style although inside a succession of alterations are visible including the addition of a second storey. At the bottom is a garden with a huge picture of the countryside.

48: House of the Silver Wedding. Built during the Samnite era, this was altered during the period of Roman imperialism. The vast tetrastyle *atrium*, the peristyle and the garden with its open-air *triclinium* are remarkable.

49: The House of Menander. This house belonged to one of the largest families in Pompeii. Besides the master house, which had its own baths, there was a farmyard with an adjoining cowshed. It is famous for the silver treasures which were found there.

50–51: The House of Theatre Scenes. A small house situated in the *Via dell' Abbondanza*. In the *atrium* are tasteful decorations in the third Pompeiian style consisting of scenes from some comedies and tragedies.

53

54

52–54: House of the Large Fountain. Its particular speciality is the large fountain in the centre of the garden. The water spurts from a large recess decorated with mosaics and multi-coloured glass. Two theatrical masks in marble and a bronze statuette complete the picture.

55: House of M. Lucretius Fronto. An elegant building from the first imperial era. The main interest here is derived from its murals, which are in the third Pompeiian style, its mythological paintings, and above all the garden which, with its recess decorated with mosaics and its marble statuettes spread out among the grass and flowers, is particularly attractive.

55

56

57

56–57: The House of the Vettii. This is the most outstanding example of the kind of house used by the affluent class in Pompeii during the town's last few years. It belonged to two brothers who were wealthy merchants, Aulus Vettius Restitutus and Aulus Vettius Conviva. After the earthquake of 62 it was substantially renovated and decorated with ebullient murals in the fourth Pompeiian style. The spacious *atrium* opens on to a huge peristyle, with a garden decorated with fountains and small marble and bronze sculptures. Surrounding it are the living quarters, one wing of the house being reserved for women.

58–59: The portico leads directly into two rooms where the murals are remarkable for their perspective and their mythological scenes. In the first, on red backgrounds, are representations of Daedalus and Pasiphae, Ixion bound to the wheel, Dionysos and Ariadne; in the second, on yellow grounds, are pictures of Hercules strangling the serpents, the slaying of Pentheus, and the punishment of Dirce.

60

60–61: The huge hall of the *triclinium* is justly famous for its refined murals, which are on a red background and separated by pilasters embellished with maenads and satyrs. Along the frame of the plinth runs a black band showing little cherubs going about a variety of every-day tasks. The inner area is divided into compartments with various decorations.

61

73

74

73: The Villa of Mysteries. This house stands outside Pompeii at a short distance from the Herculanean gate. Inside it is large and well spaced out. It consists of living quarters around the *atrium* and the *tablinum* and on the side of the peristyle are outbuildings together with the kitchen, the oven and the cellar. Built in the second century, it was altered and restored and was for a while part of the imperial estate.

74: The Dionysian Frieze. In the hall of the *triclinium*, which is the central point of interest of the building, is a huge picture in the second Pompeiian style, the work of an artist from the first century BC. The subject has given rise to many different interpretations. It has a definite link with esoteric cults and appears to represent the successive phases in initiation to the Dionysian mysteries.

76

77

78

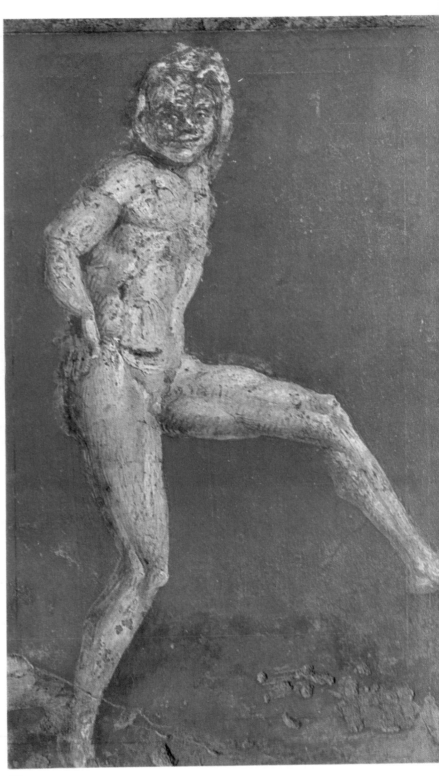

79   80

75: The reading of the ritual.
76: The terror-stricken woman.
77: Silene and Satyr.
78: The scourged woman.
79–80: Other rooms in the villa also have remarkable pictures
in the second style: a walking woman and a dancing satyr.

81

82

81: A panel which shows scenes from the sacrifice to Priapus.
82: A detail from the decoration of a *cubiculum*.

83: Villa of Julia Felix. This villa stands at the end of the *Via dell' Abbondanza.* The living quarters are decorated with a huge garden, porticos, bowers and fountains. There is also a bath and more buildings which the proprietor used to let.

84: Villa of Diomede. This stands outside the Herculanean Gate. The part used as living quarters faces a huge garden which is ornamented with fountains and sunken bowers, and overlooks the Sarno plain and the sea.

85–86: The House of Rufus. This is still in course of excavation and restoration and can be seen to be large and complicated. It is perhaps the largest house discovered in Pompeii. Built on the city walls in the first year of the Empire, it covers an extensive area and has three storeys. The side which faces the sea is imposing and has high arches in the front and a circular hall (which corresponds to a drawing room) decorated with mythological scenes on a black background. Other rooms, decorated in the fourth Pompeiian style, have already been brought to light. In addition there are baths, terraces, dressing rooms and numerous other objects and works of art.

87: A typical cross-roads with a series of arches and a public fountain.

88: The shops which adjoin the houses give a particular character to Pompeii. Here is a *thermopolium* (a tavern where drinks were served), with its counter and painted shrine, a good example of popular art.

89

89: The fullers – wool workers and washers – were numerous in Pompeii. Still extant are the wash-houses in the laundry which belonged to a certain Stephanus.

90–91: The mill-stones were worked by slaves and generally found where bread was made and sold.

90

93

92–94: The Street of Tombs. The road which leaves the Herculanean Gate, with its funereal monuments and its suburban villas, is one of the favourite places for romantic tourists. Among the curiosities are the altar at the tomb of C. Calvensius Quietus, a member of the brotherhood of Augustans, and this statue of a woman austerely clad in a coat.

94

95: **Tomb with 'exedra'** (a stone bench for visitors). Of the priestess Mamia; and a small round funereal temple which belonged to the family Istacidii.

96: The cemetery situated at the Gate of Nucera, just outside the walls, has recently been discovered. Here there are funereal monuments of various styles of architecture, often decorated with inscriptions, busts and statues of the dead.

97–98: Two typical monuments: a chapel with composite pillars and Corinthian capitals, and a circular tomb on a square base.

99: The tomb of Vestorius Priscus, outside the Vesuvius Gate, is decorated inside with paintings depicting the life of the deceased. On this panel there is a table with some pieces of crockery.

100: The tragic destiny of the Pompeiians is faithfully evoked by the bodies of the victims and by the postures which show just how they were overcome by the disaster. This is made possible by means of a special process of moulding.

101–102: Crockery and utensils of glass and bronze, chosen from among the numerous pieces discovered during the excavations, show the refined craftsmanship apparent even in the most everyday objects.

103

104

103: Statue of the Empress Livia in ceremonial attire, discovered in the Villa of Mysteries; this was for a time a part of the imperial estate.

104: The ornamental front of a sanctuary found outside the town where a Dionysian cult was celebrated. It shows Dionysos and Aphrodite.

105: Marcellus, the nephew of Augustus.

106: A Pompeiian citizen from the noble and influential family of the Poppei.

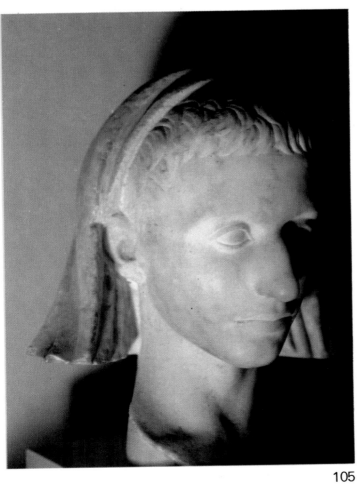

105   106

107

108

107–108: The panorama of the excavations at Pompeii reveals a different charm at various times of the day. One view of the *Via dell' Abbondanza* is in the morning and the other near sunset.

109

109: Herculaneum. A view of the excavation area from above, i.e. from the level of modern Herculaneum, showing the characteristics of this archaeological site. The town slopes towards the coast which, in ancient times, must have been nearer the centre than it is now. The regular nature of the street plan (and consequently that of the buildings) can also be seen, as can the state of repair of the ruins, which are quite high, and the not uncommon upper storeys. The harmony between old and new is also clear and shows how the new town was built on the site of the buried one.

110

111

110–112: On the southern edge vast, luxurious residences stand in rows, enjoying a magnificent panorama. They are built on the site where the boundary walls ran, made superfluous because of the security enjoyed by Campania in the first century of the Empire, and therefore demolished. All that remains is the lower part, comprising a curtain wall which served as a substructure and at the same time supported the natural cliff which was sheer at this point.

In this wall the gates between the urban centre and the outside world can be seen, set at right angles to the streets. The gates are modest and of restricted size and have no particular architectural pretensions. In one of them the wooden door is still preserved. It was this southern side that linked the town with the harbour and the sea, but also with the suburbs. In fact, in the last years of Herculaneum's existence, the town spread beyond the walls, at least to judge from the results of excavations, to the south and close to the natural border. Here a shrine was found with sacred and other objects probably connected with religious practice, and a large bath-house. Between the two blocks there is an enclosed space in which a boundary stone with a long honorary inscription and a statue, with only the base and head left, had been placed in memory of M. Nonius Balbus. He was one of the best known and most influential citizens of Herculaneum and had occupied various public posts and also been proconsul.

But from this first glimpse of ancient Herculaneum, the visitor begins to realise the characteristics of the town's topography. Next to the large house, along *cardo V* **(112)**, with its communication gate to the suburbs, there are rows of smaller houses. In this type of construction we can see a certain variety, indicative of a fairly high economic and social standard. A middle type of house, an example of a middle standard of living, is found on *cardo V*. Besides the ground floor, this house **(111)** has another two storeys with stairs, and rooms lit by windows overlooking the street.

113

114

115

113–115: Private houses and other buildings in Herculaneum were constructed along the town's streets in neat, but not monotonous, rows and their entrances give directly onto the street. On the front elevations traces of arcades with pillars or other wall supports can often be seen, but there must also have been wooden supports, of which few signs remain. Porticos were erected to give a certain architectural variety to the facade, a certain distinction to this or that house, but were also useful as protection against bad weather or excessive summer heat, a characteristic even in more recent Mediterranean building.

The streets in the urban network meet at right angles, with those running north to south being rather straight and narrow, that is *cardines* (**112**, *cardo IV*), the others, that is the *decumani*, intersecting the *cardines*, being wider and more regular. They are usually paved with trachyte stone from Vesuvius, cut into large, irregular slabs, as found in Pompeii and still to be found in Naples today. But, in some places a type of clear, calcareous stone is used, a substance of higher quality and value which was intended to give a particular importance to a certain stretch of the road. However, the ruts in the roads caused by intense cart traffic are absent in Herculaneum, while they are evident in the ancient roads of Pompeii; also lacking in Herculaneum are the stepping stones to facilitate crossing the streets on wet days. This can be explained by Herculaneum's location, situated on a slope, which did not allow for widespread use of carts and chariots and also afforded natural drainage.

At the same time, traffic could not have been as heavy in Herculaneum, which was an agricultural and holiday centre, as it was in Pompeii, which was a centre of trade and commerce. Sidewalks, sometimes low, sometimes quite high (**114**) line the streets and there are public fountains here and there at crossroads. The town's water supply would appear to have been well maintained and the fountains are very simple (**115**): a trough made with slabs of calcareous stone and a decorative mask at the mouth.

116

116–120: Decumanus Maximus. The main street, running to the centre of the urban network, was the *Decumanus Maximus*, which was very wide and reserved exclusively for pedestrians. It must have had the same purpose in daily life and in the town's political and economic life as the Forum, which is common in other ancient towns but is absent in Herculaneum. Facing the *decumanus* we find some of the most beautiful houses, such as the House of the Bicentenary which achieved great notoriety when the traces of a Christian cross could be seen on the plaster of a small room on the top floor; we find shops and artisans' workshops with painted signs, various pieces of earthenware and tools.

Excavations during the last ten years have

revealed an extremely interesting block **(117–118)**, along the northern side. On the front runs a portico with columns and pillars of brick and the portico is also lit by small windows opening above the intercolumns. Above, there are at least two floors of accommodation.

Behind the portico are the entrances to houses and shops but, unfortunately, it is not possible to go beyond these entrances because houses of modern Herculaneum have been built on top of them. An accurate excavation and a delicate piece of workmanship have led to the recovery of wooden construction elements, the horizontal girder holding the cover of the portico **(120)**, the door jambs, the door knockers, the flat arches and window shutters **(119)**.

To the east of the block, similarly unearthed, rises one of the greatest public buildings in Herculaneum, the Basilica. We are familiar with the plan, drawn by excavators of the Bourbon period while exploring it by means of subterranean tunnels. It is a vast, rectangular area terminating at the back with three apses, and divided longitudinally by two rows of columns. The walls had ornate paintings. We know of three of them, depicting mythological themes with the myths of Theseus and the Minotaur, Achilles and Chiron, Hercules and Telephus; the paintings are of Hellenistic inspiration. Bronze statues were also found. The paintings and sculptures from this excavation are now at the archaeological museum in Naples.

117

118

119   120

121–122: Two water-fountains on the *Decumanus Maximus*.

123: Two four-fronted brick arches flanked the facade of the Basilica, and were set the entire width of the *decumanus*. Of these only one has been completely unearthed with fragments of its delicate stucco decoration, geometric figures and motifs, covering the inside walls. In front of the Basilica, but on the edge of the street, there is a brick porch, decorated in stucco and marble. Here and there in the intervening space are the remains of plinths of bronze statues which were undoubtedly in honour of notable Herculanean citizens and members of the family. Some fragments are still fixed to the base which show how there must also have been equestrian groups. It should be remembered that the sculptures had already been recovered at the time of the Bourbon excavations and that they should, therefore, be identified with some of the bronze sculptures, either whole or in fragments, which are in the Archaeological Museum of Naples.

To the south of the *decumanus* a large public building has been partly identified, walls regularly spaced with half columns, while to the east a monumental entrance to the upper hall of the great gymnasium opens on to the *decumanus*.

124: The small building to the south of the *Decumanus Maximus* is a departure from the usual architectural design. It is square with a covering supported by four pillars, similar to the tetrastyle *atrium* of a private house. But in the background a smaller area has been unearthed, which is elegantly decorated with marble flagstones and paintings, where the central theme is Hercules, the eponymous hero of the town. From its structure and some texts found there, the building has been identified either as a place dedicated to the imperial cult or as a meeting place for the town's magistrates (*curia*), or even as both. But it was probably the public *Lararium*, a place or worship analogous with one found in Pompeii.

125

126

127

128

125–128: The Great Gymnasium. Impressive and architecturally highly developed is the great gymnasium **(125–126),** which has still only been partly excavated. The main part, from what we can see, is a vast open air section in the centre of which is a large swimming pool with four arms, which was added to or replaced a smaller one found a short distance away. Along at least two sides, and possibly three, ran a colonnade. Behind the western door **(127)** a number of different areas open out, among which is a large apsed hall **(128).** This has a marble floor with a table in the centre where winners were honoured, a large rectangular room, dedicated perhaps to the worship of Esculapius and Hygieia, gods of good health, while other areas must have been connected with athletic activities which took place in the sports ground. On this side there is also a monumental vestibule opening onto *cardo V*. But, apart from this entrance, the entire front of the block of buildings along the *cardo* had no other connection with the sports ground because we find private houses and shops there.

The block of the sports ground is on two levels. The upper one connects with the *Decumanus Maximus*; here, too, there is a monumental entrance which leads to a grandiose rectangular hall and thence to other large rooms situated along a colonnade.

129–133: Town Baths. In classical times the gymnasium played a very important part in the town's life. It was a place where athletes trained and prepared for athletic competitions and where the youths came to care for their bodies with all kinds of gymnastic exercise. This type of building, with its special functions, was common in Greece and later became part of Roman life where it was highly developed. It is not strange, therefore, that a small place like Herculaneum should have had such a big, impressive sports centre. Also very much part of Roman life were the bath-houses which, in a certain sense, had similar functions to that of the sports ground and took over some of them. In Herculaneum there are two bath-houses of which the oldest is situated between the *cardines* III and IV, along the *Decumanus Inferior*. This dates from the Augustan era but was restored at various times afterwards.

As is customary in such buildings, the bath-houses are divided into a section for men (**129–130**), which is the bigger section, and a section for women (**132–135**). The men's section is entered from *cardo* III. The changing room (*apodyterium*) has seats and corbels for clothes running the whole way around. The *frigidarium* (**129**) is a round tub for cold baths and is painted with marine fauna. The *tepidarium* and *calidarium* (**130**) follow the *frigidarium*; they were designed to enable bathing in two different temperatures. The Romans did this either by immersion or by steam (as in a Turkish bath); hot air circulated in the space between the two floors placed one on top of the

other, of which the upper one is supported by terracotta columns (*suspensurae*); sometimes the walls have cavities which serve the same purpose.

In the *tepidarium* the floor is a mosaic with a Triton surrounded by four dolphins, in the *calidarium* there is also a bath tub and a wash basin. The women's section, as is usual in Roman bath-houses, is the same as the men's, with its entrance on the side of the *cardo* IV. In the changing room (132), there is a mosaic floor with the same theme of the Triton, here depicted with a rudder on his shoulder, surrounded by a cupid, four nymphs, an octopus and a cuttle-fish. The decoration of the *tepidarium* and *calidarium* are simpler (133). The heating apparatus serves both sections; the water is kept in large tanks and is heated to evaporation point and the hot air is circulated. A small gymnasium (131) completes the building's installation. It is an uncovered area with a portico on three sides and some small annexes. Athletic training could be done here while another space, possibly roofed, was a 'bowl' for ball games.

134–136: Suburban Bath-houses. The suburban
bath-houses, though smaller, are very interesting
and are found immediately outside the urban
area and date from the last period of Herculaneum's
existence. The facade, with a door and low windows of very simple design, rises on the space
enclosing the honorary monument of M. Nonius
Balbus and this area also acts as an entrance
courtyard to the baths. Inside, the layout is
compact and unusual. Beyond the entrance and
down some steps there is the vestibule **(135)**
which is shaped like a tetrastyle *atrium*. On the
pillars there are arches, and some flat arches, on
which rests a second row of arches and the area is
lit directly from above, subtly diffusing the light
between the architectural components. The various
sections of the building lead off from here.

Next to the entrance there is a room lit by
large windows, a rest room for the customers'
comfort. From the front of the entrance there is a
huge area which is both changing room (*apodyterium*) and *frigidarium* **(135)**. Here a large part of
the room is occupied by the cold water bath tub.
By the side of the *frigidarium* there is another
unusual area **(136),** with marble and stucco
decoration and with marble seats all around the
walls. This serves as a waiting room with access
either to the *frigidarium* or to a part of the *tepidarium*
on one side or the *calidarium* on the other. Of
these two the *tepidarium* has a large pool (*natatio*)
and is linked to a small, round room used for sweat
baths (*laconicum*), while the *calidarium* is provided
with a small tub and a wash basin. Behind the
calidarium there is the boiler room (*praefurnium*)
which, in its turn, leads to the vestibule. Finally,
there is a long service corridor skirting the block
on the north side. The absence of a gymnasium
gives a compact area which is lit by windows or
skylights.

There is widespread use of stucco decorating
the walls and also marble, either white or coloured,
used as a wall covering and floor decoration.
Wooden objects have also been excavated which
still function, in some cases, as they used to do.

Scattered materials, such as wooden beams and
brick, reveal that restoration work was still in
progress at the time of the eruption. These bath-
houses do not have separate sections for men and
women, and it is probable that there were different
bathing times for each sex.

137: House of Aristides. The House of Aristides, on the southern edge of the town, was explored during the eighteenth century using the underground tunnel method, which caused structural damage to the most important house in this district, The Villa of Papyri. The building is supported by a strong substructure which extends beyond the natural edge and makes use of the former defence wall and the internal embankment in which some subterranean areas were unearthed.

The house is entered from *cardo* III through a door which, fronted by a porch on the sidewalk, leads directly into the *atrium*, which is unusual. The various rooms, whose purpose it is difficult to identify, are built on two axes at right angles. There is a long colonnade on the most southern tip.

From a technical and functional point of view, the substructures are very interesting, with a brick front and arched passages leading into the basement areas. These partially covered passages are of very sound structure and are approached from a small internal staircase.

The House of Aristides dates from the last years of Herculaneum's existence.

138: The House of the Hotel. This is the largest of the villas and is located in the southern part of the town. Its design is original and has given rise to its traditional, though erroneous name. It was built in the Augustan era and was later rebuilt and modified. It opens on to *cardo* IV and on this side, along the walls of the *atrium*, there are a series of rooms with various uses in everyday life. There is also a bathing area with a *praefurnium*, a changing room, *tepidarium* and *calidarium*. Behind the block there is the peristyle with an arcade; its four sides surround the garden and orchard, which are situated on a lower level than the arcade.

The southern side of the peristyle connects a group of rooms of which the central one would have been the *tablinum*. These rooms in turn open above another large four-sided arcade whose end is used as a terrace and belvedere. Here the house stands on a substructure which serves as a living room.

Some parts of the house have signs which indicate later changes, giving the impression that the house lost its original patrician character and became a merchant's house. This can frequently be seen in the houses of Pompeii, but less so in Herculaneum, and must be connected with the change in the social and economic structure of these towns in the years between the earthquake of 62 and the eruption in 79.

139–144: House of the Mosaic Atrium. Entering the house from *cardo* IV and crossing the vestibule, one comes to the *atrium*. This is of the 'Tuscan' type and has a beautiful floor with a simple, geometrical mosaic consisting of black and white squares. Today it is very uneven: volcanic matter which poured down on it has made the surface give way, because of older buildings buried under the floor itself. After this comes the *tablinum*, divided as it were into three aisles of two rows of pillars with windows set high up in the walls, which give a great deal of light to the area. It is a design reminiscent of the Basilica and, in a private house, is unusual from an architectural point of view.

The sequence of these 'public' rooms is as usual for private Roman houses of the *atrium* type, but there are no surrounding accommodation quarters. The rest of the house, as in the House of the Hotel, extends at right angles to this first

139

140

group of rooms, either because of the space
available or the view enjoyed at the southern
edge of the town. We find on this side a windowed
arcade (141) to which access is gained from the
atrium, and which encloses a garden (140). Along
the arcade on the eastern side, there are living
rooms, the side ones being smaller than the central
ones. The ceilings and walls have elegant pictorial
decorations, with small pictures in the centre
where a mythological scene (the torment of
Dirce, Diana bathing) has been inserted. To the
south are living quarters: a large room in the
centre with living rooms to the side, which are
very extravagantly decorated with wall paintings
and marble floors. The extreme end of the house
is entirely taken up by a covered colonnade and a
panoramic terrace (139). At the end of the
terrace there are a further two living rooms,
particularly suitable for admiring the view in this
mild climate, *cubicula diurna* as they are called by
Latin writers, who frequently refer to them.
Much of the woodwork has been preserved in
place and as it actually was: door and window
frames, ceiling supports and joists. A cradle and
small table were also found intact (143) which,
besides their value and rarity, enable the visitor
to have a clearer idea of daily life in the middle of
the first century AD.

141

143

142

144

145

144–151: The House of the Stags. This belongs to the series of panoramic houses described, but also evidences a later development in the design of the traditional kind of house, and new standards of luxury and architectural innovation. The evolution of design is not chronological because the house dates from the time of Claudius-Nero with some later restoration work after the earthquake of 62. The house is on *cardo V* with the usual entrance and vestibule, and then develops almost entirely in a longitudinal direction running north to south. The *atrium* has been reduced to minimal proportions and is not distinguishable from any other room and does not have an opening in the roof (*compluvium*), nor the usual *impluvium* tank. A number of rooms, including the kitchen and larder, are adjacent to the *atrium* and a French window opens southwards. The arcade closely resembles that of the House of the Mosaic Atrium, but they differ from each other in detail. The arcade in the House of the Stags has four sides and surrounds the garden and the section containing the two large living rooms. The house ends on this side with a colonnade, which has been made more comfortable by a *pergula* and *cubicula diurna* (**144**). The house is richly and elegantly decorated. The mural paintings are of the fourth style with its characteristic lively and fantastic themes, and they stand out with their linear designs on a black background (**144–147**).

146

147

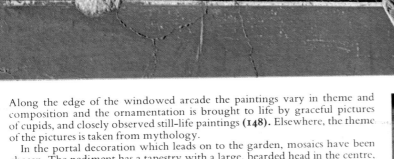

Along the edge of the windowed arcade the paintings vary in theme and composition and the ornamentation is brought to life by graceful pictures of cupids, and closely observed still-life paintings (148). Elsewhere, the theme of the pictures is taken from mythology.

In the portal decoration which leads on to the garden, mosaics have been chosen. The pediment has a tapestry with a large, bearded head in the centre, a personification of Oceanus, and at each side a frieze of cupids riding on seahorses (145). Much of the floors remains; these are sometimes simple mosaics (149), with marble in the more important rooms.

The house gets its name from two sculptured groups, which both represent a stag being attacked by dogs as in the lower illustration on the following page (151). Both these compositions show the artist's inventive skill in the treatment of an animalistic theme and also his virtuosity in marble work. To the mythical world, or rather to a good-humoured, not to say comic, interpretation of that world, belongs the satyr with the wine-skin (150) and the inebriated Silenus, and here too we can admire the grace of the theme and the interplay of anatomy.

15

150

151

152: The House of Argus. Eighteenth century exploration and later excavations at the beginning of the nineteenth century brought to light only a part of what must have been one of the most beautiful patrician residences in Herculaneum, the House of Argus. From what we know, we can assume that it was next to the House of Aristides and occupied a large area; it follows the same pattern as the rich, luxurious houses in the southern part of the town. It must have had two entrances on the west with a secondary one on *cardo* III; the latter entrance is elegantly set in the facade and has a front porch extending on to the pavement. Inside, there is a solemn, monumental peristyle, colonnaded on three sides, with columns and pillars in stucco; the back leads into the dining room (*triclinium*).

Of another adjoining peristyle only a small section has been excavated. But at the time of its discovery apartments, and larders containing charred foodstuffs, were found on the upper floor. This floor overlooked the street and was supported by buttresses which have unfortunately been lost and they are known to us only by descriptions and drawings of the time.

153–154: The Samnite House. This gives a clear example of a private house in pre-Roman Herculaneum.

The house dates from the latter half of the second century BC and the plan and distribution of rooms and much of its decorative work still remain as they originally were. At the front there is the entrance **(153)** with an elegant portal in tufa blocks, Corinthian capitals and a dentile cornice. In the vestibule the decoration of the first style still remains with painted embossed stucco. The *atrium*, in imitation marble, is beautifully proportioned and in its original form. At the top there is a loggia with Ionic columns and trellis woodwork; the loggia is partly ornamental and partly functional and is an imitation of Hellenistic architecture. Even the floors in 'cocciopesto' (beaten clay), belong to the first phase of construction. There is an upper storey with two small apartments, one of which can be reached from the ground floor, thus forming an integral part of the house itself, but the other apartment is independent with an external staircase leading to it. In some of the rooms, paintings of the second and fourth styles indicate restoration work done to mural decoration in the house.

153 154

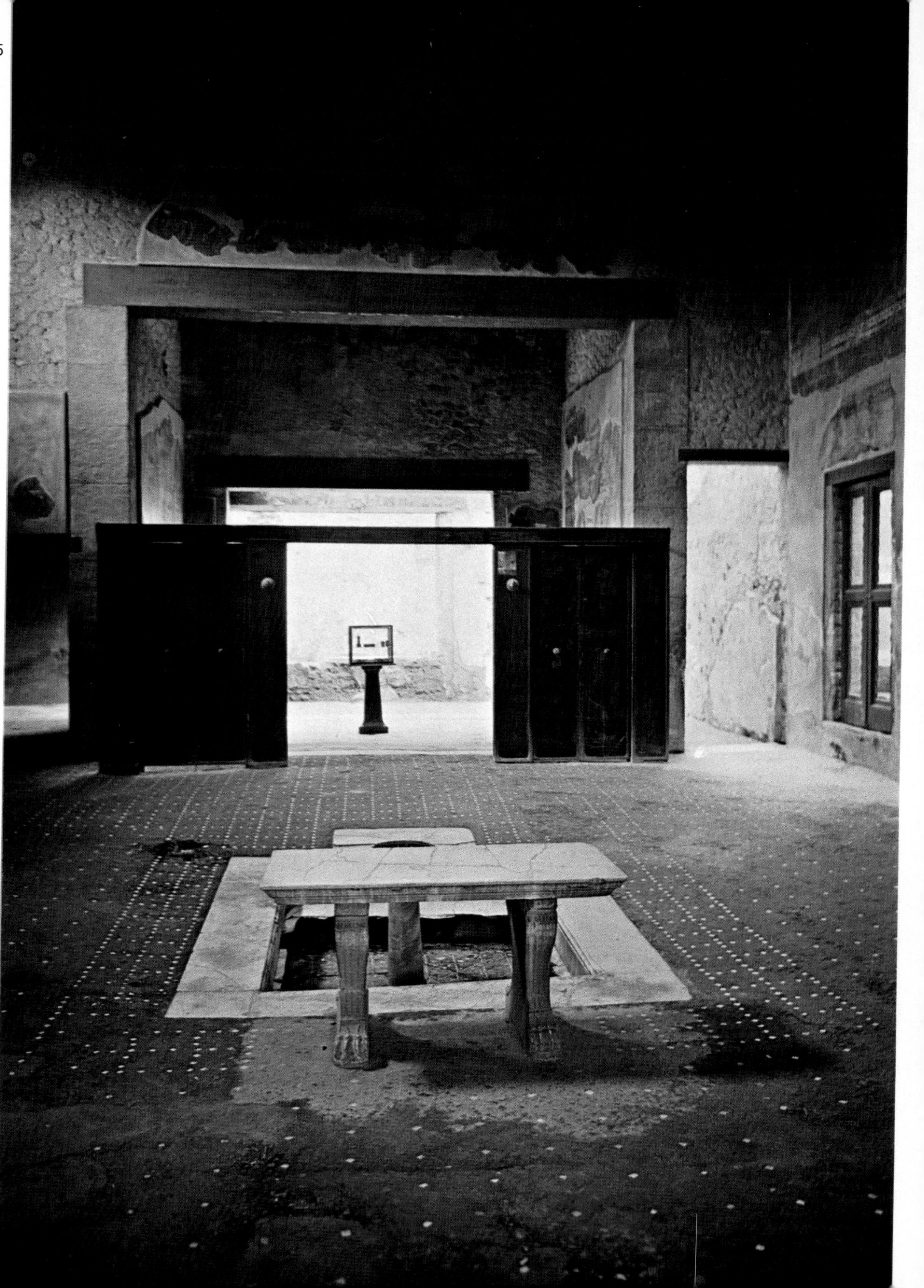

155–156: House of the Wooden Partition. This house also dates from the Samnite period and its original appearance has largely been preserved. Later, however, towards the middle of the first century of the Empire, it underwent various changes and was extended to create other rooms (or incorporated some from adjoining houses). An upper floor was built, whilst the rooms on the *Decumanus Inferior* (**156**) were converted into shops; other rooms were divided into more apartments. This is interesting in that it shows the transitional period from the patrician *domus* to rented houses accommodating more than one family; the change is due either to different social conditions or the demands of urban life. The name of the house comes from the wooden partition dividing the *atrium* from the *tablinum* (**155**).

157: House of the Two Atria. The need to make better use of the limited space available where there are public buildings, the Baths and large houses, determined the unusual design of the House of the Two Atria. It is long and narrow and has a first *atrium* just past the entrance and the vestibule; this *atrium* is of the tetrastyle kind and is followed by the *tablinum*, as is customary. But after this there is a second *atrium* with a large room opening off it at the back. The living rooms are only along one side of this block. On the ground floor the entrance portal has an architrave in tufa. On the upper floor the rooms are lit by windows and a brick cornice marks the division between floors; on the top there are traces of roof beams.

158: House of the Great Portal. Another example of the use of space and distribution of rooms differing from the norm can be seen in this house, which dates from between 62 and 79 AD. The entrance portal, from which the house gets its name, is worth noting for its brickwork and half pillars, architrave and latticed cornice. In contrast, the Corinthian capitals are of stone with figures of winged Victories. The *atrium* is replaced by a vestibule, which is very long and runs across the building and which also acts as the centrepoint of the house. To the south this connects with an uncovered courtyard and a room, and to the north the *triclinium*, with various rooms, including the kitchen, leading off it. The wall paintings are in the fourth style.

Along the walls of the vestibule there are columns in tufa inserted into the structure, probably belonging to a building pre-dating the present house, rather than used as a construction material.

157

158

159: House of the Beautiful Courtyard.
Another example of the variety of design in
Herculaneum's private houses, this comprises a
beautiful courtyard on two levels. On the ground
floor the entrance room is long and low with small
rustic rooms on one side. This leads into the
courtyard, of harmonious proportions, from
which there is an open staircase with a parapet
and balcony leading to the upper storey. This is a
very practical architectural solution to separating
the various sections of the house and recalls a
type of Italian building widespread in the Middle
Ages and the Renaissance and even in present day
country houses. On the side of the courtyard there
is a huge sitting room decorated with paintings
of the fourth style. On the upper floor there is
another group of apartments with a wooden
balcony overlooking the street.

160–161: House of the Relief of Telephus.
In the variety of Herculanean buildings, the
House of the Relief of Telephus has a special
position. In one way, it resembles the luxurious
villas on the southern edge of the town, yet in
another some design adaptation was necessary
because of the uneven terrain.

In the main block of buildings along *cardo* V,
there is an entrance to a large vestibule and then
into an *atrium* of unusual shape, resembling the
colonnade courtyards of private houses in ancient
Greece. The area is surrounded by a portico **(160)**

161

which revolves around a huge space. Above, the rooms of the upper storey face inwards with a balcony and above that the roof. In the centre is the *impluvium* which is a square tank with high edges. Walls and columns are painted in a beautiful shade of bright red. At the back of the *atrium* is the *tablinum*, while to the left there is a rustic area with a series of rooms, of which the most interesting is the stable (*stabulum*). In this section of the house there is a sloping corridor which runs alongside the *tablinum*.

Here a peristyle with brick columns surrounds a spacious garden with a large, rectangular trough in the centre **(161)**. Three rooms open off the peristyle and across another corridor there is a group of rooms forming the southern extremity of the entire block. In these rooms, which probably had different uses, such as reception, rest and dining rooms, the multi-coloured marble work is worth noting. They have geometric and architectural designs and decorated walls and floors, which is a sign of exceptional wealth and good taste. A similar standard of luxury and an abundant use of marble is found in rooms which, because of the overhanging earth, have been excavated in a floor underneath this. The house was also decorated with works of art which were salvaged from the volcanic downpour which must have carried many things much further, and lower down there is a relief of neo-Greek art in which the myth of Telephus is depicted and a group of *oscilla* in marble which decorated the *atrium*.

162

162–163: House of Charred Furniture. We have already mentioned that pieces of structure, furniture and wooden objects have been recovered in Herculaneum and it is precisely from these that the house gets its name, that is, from charred furniture. The house is simple and traditional in design and dates from pre-Roman times but had later additions made to it which did not, however, affect its original appearance. It is decorated with wall paintings (163) of the third and fourth styles. Behind the *tablinum* there is a small garden and a shrine to the Lares with graceful, architectural lines (162).

164: House of the Tuscan Colonnade. Beautiful and spacious houses stand along the main street of Herculaneum. That of the Tuscan colonnade was built in the Samnite period with large tufa blocks characteristic of the time, and was rebuilt in the first half of the imperial era and restored after the earthquake of 62 AD. It retained its original appearance, although two rooms on street level were converted into shops. The *atrium, tablinum* and their adjacent rooms are traditional in style; the house then widens with a magnificent peristyle which, with its elegant Tuscan colonnade, has given its name to the house. Around the peristyle there are various rooms, as in the great patrician villas. The wall paintings follow the phases of structural restoration because they have walls in the third and fourth styles. A store of gold coins, the only ones ever found in Herculaneum, testify to the inhabitants' wealth.

165: House of the Bicentenary. This house, too, follows the usual design of the *domus* but on a spacious plan and, situated as it is along the main street of the town, the *Decumanus Maximus*, must have belonged to some of the most important families in Herculaneum. During the last part of the town's existence, however, some rooms on the ground floor were converted into shops because of new social and economic conditions. But, apart from the interest arising from the elegance of its design, the House of the Bicentenary has achieved fame for a very different reason. In a room on the upper floor, in the servants' quarters, a frame in the shape of a cross inside a white stucco panel has been found. It is thought that the casing housed a wooden cross, symbol of the Christian religion which may have been practised by someone in the household. If this was so, it would indicate that the cult of the Cross dates much earlier among Christians than was supposed.

166–167: The Trellis House. This house constitutes a good example of constructional development from the *domus* with an *atrium*, used for just one family, to the type of house with several apartments, which were rented to different families. This aspect of Roman building is well documented in Ostia during the first period of the Empire, but here we have a rare example of it, dating from the preceding era. The house is constructed of a wooden frame filled with

166

167

rubble and is of poor, superficial technique. In the centre are a courtyard acting as a source of light, stairs and a corridor which separate the different apartments on the ground and upper floors; the facade is fronted by a portico supporting a loggia (166). In one of the rooms there are the charred remains of a cupboard (167).

16

168–171: The House of Neptune. This is of very simple design on two floors and reveals a particularly refined taste on the part of the owner, who ran a shop on the street front, which communicated with the house itself **(168)**; the front part of the house was on *cardo* III. Various fragments of good quality painted decoration remain; at the back of the *atrium* there is not only the *tablinum* but also a room which could have been used as a reception or dining room, and a small, uncovered courtyard. This is the richest and most interesting part of the house. In the centre there is a *triclinium* in stone covered with marble **(171)**; and on one wall there is a mosaic representing Neptune and Amphytrite **(172)**, with a shell design above. On another wall is a *nymphaeum*, with a central apsed niche and two rectangular niches on each side. This is decorated in mosaics depicting various themes of life, with festoons of leaves and fruit, and hunting scenes with fleeing stags and dogs. The mosaic decoration of the courtyard is very fresh and rich in colour, but is above all a rare example of that mosaic wall ornamentation which was widespread in classical times, but has been almost completely lost.

The rooms on the upper floor are well preserved, with their wall paintings and various pieces of furniture. The shop, recovered practically intact, is impressive. We find the counter with earthenware and other everyday articles and urns inside which there are still grain and other scorched foodstuffs, a wooden rack where amphorae are kept **(169)**, and the hearth and sink. It is a scene that immediately captures the imagination with its commercial but humble atmosphere, which is typical of Herculanean life.

172–176: Shops. If we glance at the places of commercial activity, which we shall call shops for simplicity's sake, we find things of interest everywhere. These, in fact, are a faithful reflection of customs, economic and social conditions in the town at the time of its burial. We have already seen how these shops multiplied in the years preceding the eruption for reasons which we can guess at, even if only to a limited extent. Among these reasons was greater wealth enabling more intensive production, an economy based on trade as opposed to a traditional economy based on agriculture, and an increase in industrial activity within the limits of the age.

Many 'shops', as we have seen, are situated where there used to be a patrician *domus*, others form part of the body of a house owned by the shopkeeper. There are obviously many different kinds of commercial activity. For food, for instance, we have the *pistrina* which produced and sold bread, shops selling agricultural produce, such as the House of Neptune, oil and wine shops, *thermopolia* and *tabernae*, similar to our bars and taverns. In all these places archaeological excava-

172

173

5

6

tion has brought to light relevant paraphernalia, as for example, counters and shelves and, behind the shop or in the connecting rooms, beds and seats. The proprietor's religious inclination was sometimes revealed by the presence of a shrine to the Lares where the household gods were worshipped. Moreover, abundant articles, such as jugs, glasses, amphorae, vats and all kinds of earthenware have been found. Also found are oil lamps, sometimes in terracotta, sometimes in bronze, and various types of charred foodstuffs such as grain, vegetables and fruit. There is a great variety of businesses and workshops and there are shops selling a wide range of goods, from cloth to bronze articles and glassware. We have the unusual example of a tavern displaying a painted sign on the entrance; here, apart from the name of the tavern and the god under whose protection it is, we find a list of what is available and the price. Inscriptions often found on furniture have given us a great deal of information about the names of people, addresses, types of cloth, etc. and also texts and graffiti painted on walls.

172: Corner shop with accommodation.

173–174: Detail of a shop on the upper *cardo* V and charred bed at the back of the shop.

175–176: Tavern on the corner of the *Decumanus Inferior* and *cardo* V, the pots on the counter being protected by a glass display case.

177–186: Stabiae. Villa of San Marco. This has not been completely excavated and part of it must be considered as lost forever because of erosion of the mountain spur on which it stands. However, it reveals an impressive design in which can be distinguished various interconnecting sections on different levels, to make most use of the terrain. At the centre is the *atrium* **(178),** which opens on one side of the block and around which the various rooms are situated. From here, across a small portico, there is the bath-house, which is particularly large in comparison to others in private villas and houses. Around a colonnaded *atrium*, the different sections of the bath-house can be seen including the *calidarium*, the *tepidarium* and the *frigidarium* **(179).** Beyond, to the west, there is a garden area (it appears that rows of plane-trees were planted there among others) with a pool taking up the central part for the length of the garden **(180).** At the end looking out over the sea the garden leads, by way of one arm of the portico,

into a large salon and minor rooms. At the opposite end it is bordered by the slightly curving facade of a covered gallery. The long sides of the garden are flanked partially by the two wings of the portico and in part by two symmetrical groups of rooms, slightly raised above the garden, suitable for repose and siestas and decorated with elegant and airy murals. Adjoining the garden further to the west is another uncovered area in which there must have been a colonnade of which now only a portion remains. In this colonnade it is worth noting the stucco decoration on the columns. The pictorial decorations which have been recovered from various parts of the villa are of high quality: figures rendered in a lively impressionistic style, with a deft play of shadow and light, and subtle linear motifs that divide lower walls, on which appear detailed miniatures and even

181: Shrine of the household gods. **182**: First peristyle. **183**: Wall frescoes of the fourth style

countryside scenes with buildings, one of which is a view of the villa itself. The back wall of the first garden is decorated with stucco where athletic and mythical figures stand out among elaborate cornices. These painted and stucco decorations are now, for the most part, kept in the nearby Antiquarium, while those recovered in the Bourbon period are in the Naples Museum. Some items, such as two obsidian cups decorated with scenes of Egyptian influence and inlaid with gold and multi-coloured stones, show the standard of wealth and luxury of the villa.

The villa must have been constructed during the first years of the Empire, but until the catastrophe of Vesuvius was well looked after, embellished and repaired. From such an impressive building it is certain that the owner must have come from one of the most important families who visited the area. It is thought that the villa, at least for a time, must have been part of the imperial estate, a theory based on an inscription relating to Narcissus, the powerful freed slave of the Emperor Claudius.

184: Stucco of the first peristyle. **185–186:** Cupid with drum and landscape panel originating from the Villa of San Marco and kept in the Antiquarium of Castellammare di Stabia.

187–190: Stabiae. Villa of Varanus (or Villa of the Vendor of Love). This is similar to the Villa of San Marco both in the damage caused by soil erosion and in its design. But there are also individual details worth noting. The excavation has until now been done by a long and narrow trench, so that it is not clear whether the building was one, or two different villas adjacent to each other. In its present state, the structural complex is limited to the extremities of two gardens with porticos. From the west, there is a series of rooms overlooking a terrace facing the sea and supported by a buttress and blind arches **(187).** Among these it is worth noting a great sitting room with windows, perhaps a *triclinium*, a second sitting room next to which is the kitchen and a room with an apse for heating purposes. There follows another series of minor rooms around an *atrium* and yet another series of varying sizes which stretch as far as the eastern peristyle **(188).** The direction of the various rooms in the entire building is not consistent, since the uneven slope of the land must have had to be considered. However, parts of the building were subject to repairs to the original structure and later restoration work.

Here, too, wall paintings are of a high standard. Mythological pictures depict the myth of Dionysos and Ariadne and the myth of Licurgus with its clear colours. In one room, the unusual wall decoration is divided into diamond shapes, between which are mythical or allegorical figurines, birds, symbols, etc. Even from the time of the Bourbon excavations, some of the most famous and sophisticated paintings have been recovered from this villa, which are today in the Naples Museum, such as the Nereids on a red background, the group of small pictures to which belongs the famous Primavera and the scene of the Vendor of Love.

189: Ceiling panel with figures, from the Villa of Varanus, now in the Antiquarium.

190

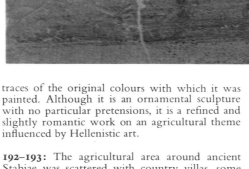

190: Fresco from the Villa of Varanus, probably representing Theseus, now in the Antiquarium.

191: In addition to these two villas, recent excavations have brought to light other and equally big villas on the hill of Varano. These were explored during the Bourbon period and still remain underground, but we know the design because of plans drawn up at the time. From one villa, between that of San Marco and that of Varanus, and which we only know in part, has come a small but valuable statue (now in the Antiquarium). It is an old shepherd, covered in rough haircloth, carrying a kid on his shoulders; in his left hand he is holding a basket of fruit and sheaves of corn and has a hare in his right hand. The marble surface still has

traces of the original colours with which it was painted. Although it is an ornamental sculpture with no particular pretensions, it is a refined and slightly romantic work on an agricultural theme influenced by Hellenistic art.

192–193: The agricultural area around ancient Stabiae was scattered with country villas, some serving as accommodation for the farmer and his wife, or as a small farm.

A villa of this sort has been discovered in the Carmiano region, with a simple yet functional design. In the centre there is an open area, an internal courtyard around which rooms are built; there are also deposits of farm produce, and service rooms. But even with its modest design, so

different from the great patrician villas of Stabiae, the Villa of Carmiano was embellished with good wall paintings. The shrine to the Lares is particularly interesting **(192)** and is now in the Antiquarium. This shrine is a miniature pavilion of stucco with a two-columned facade. On the back of the pavilion, which held small statues of the Lares and Penates, there is a painting of Minerva, seated on a throne with a helmet on her head and holding her sword and shield; the picture has a certain solemnity in spite of its small size. At the bottom of the wall there is the traditional serpent symbolising good luck to the inhabitants of the house, by the sacrificial altar.